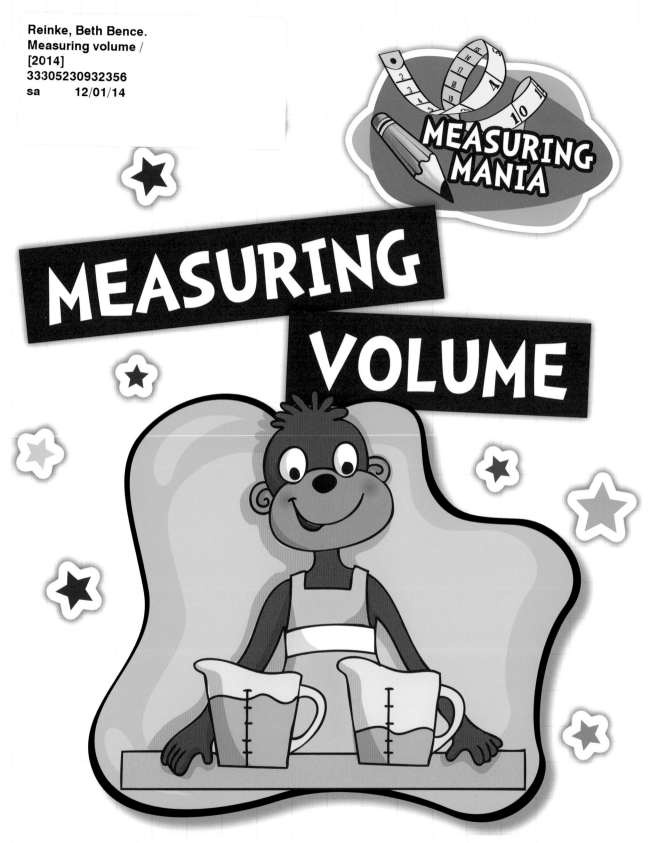

MEASURING MANIA

MEASURING VOLUME

by Beth Bence Reinke   illustrated by Kathleen Petelinsek

Published in the United States of America by Cherry Lake Publishing
Ann Arbor, Michigan
www.cherrylakepublishing.com

Consultants: Janice Bradley, PhD, Mathematically Connected Communities,
New Mexico State University; Marla Conn, ReadAbility, Inc.

Editorial direction: Red Line Editorial
Book design and illustration: The Design Lab

Photo credits: Patrick Foto/Shutterstock Images, 5; Shutterstock Images, 6, 11;
Red Line Editorial, 10; Margaret M. Stewart/Shutterstock Images, 14; Christian
de Araujo/Shutterstock Images, 21

Library of Congress Cataloging-in-Publication Data
Reinke, Beth Bence.
  Measuring volume / by Beth Bence Reinke.
    pages cm. — (Measuring mania)
  Audience: 5–8.
  Audience: K to grade 3.
  Includes bibliographical references and index.
  ISBN 978-1-62431-651-7 (hardcover) — ISBN 978-1-62431-678-4 (pbk.) —
ISBN 978-1-62431-705-7 (pdf) — ISBN 978-1-62431-732-3 (hosted ebook)
  1. Volume (Cubic content)—Juvenile literature. I. Title.
  QC104.R45 2014
  530.8'1—dc23
                          2013029075

Cherry Lake Publishing would like to acknowledge
the work of The Partnership for 21st Century Skills.
Please visit www.p21.org for more information.

Printed in the United States of America
Corporate Graphics Inc.
January 2014

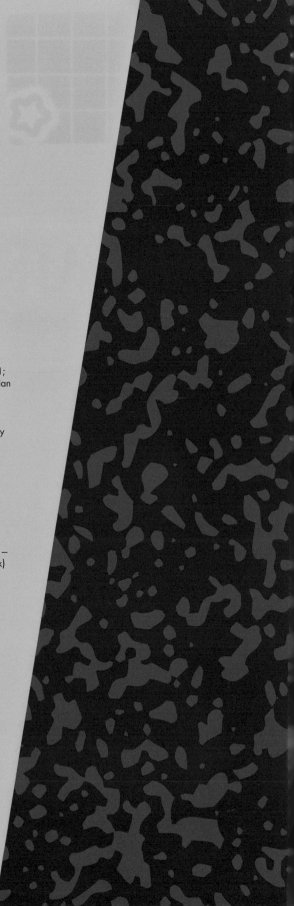

Table of Contents

CHAPTER ONE

What Is Volume?

How much water do you think your bathtub holds?

You can fill the bathtub with water. Or you can pour juice into a glass. You can scoop sand into a bucket, too.

Look at a glass of milk. Can you tell how much is in it? It's hard to know just by looking. You can measure the milk to find the **volume**. Volume is how much space something takes up. Everything big and small has volume.

Do you have a favorite glass? How much milk do you think it holds?

It can be difficult to guess how much fits in bottles of different shapes.

How much water is in a swimming pool? How much ketchup does the bottle hold? How much milk and cereal are in your bowl? You can find out. Let's measure volume!

To do the activities in this book, you will need:

- empty gallon jug
- empty quart bottle
- empty liter bottle
- **funnel**
- measuring cup
- measuring spoons
- dry rice or unpopped popcorn
- baking supplies

Gather what you need.

CHAPTER TWO

Volume Big and Small

The zookeeper measures the penguin's medicine in teaspoons.

Everything has volume. What if you have something big to measure? You need big **units** of volume. We use gallons or liters for water in a swimming pool. Gallons and liters are units of measure for liquids. Small amounts need small units. We use teaspoons or milliliters for medicine.

This list will help you remember units of volume.

- 1 gallon is the same as 4 quarts (3.8 L)
- 1 quart is the same as 2 pints (0.9 L)
- 1 pint is the same as 2 cups (0.5 L)
- 1 cup is the same as 8 fluid ounces (0.2 L)
- 1 fluid ounce is the same as 2 tablespoons (30 mL)
- 1 tablespoon is the same as 3 teaspoons (15 mL)

One quart is the same as 2 pints or 4 cups (0.5 L).

1 QUART
2 PINTS
4 CUPS

Look at a container of ice cream and a container of milk. Which has a greater volume? One is taller than the other. They are not the same shape. One might be heavier, too. But their volume is the same. The two containers take up the same amount of space.

The containers have different shapes but hold the same volume.

What happens if you add too many popcorn kernels to the pan?

ACTIVITY

Measuring Ingredients

INSTRUCTIONS:
1. Measure these amounts of dry rice or unpopped popcorn. As you measure, dump them into a big bowl.

    2 cups (same as 1 pint)

    1 cup (same as 8 fluid ounces)

    2 tablespoons (same as 1 fluid ounce)

    3 teaspoons (same as 1 tablespoon)

2. Put the food back into the box when you are finished.

To get a copy of this activity, visit www.cherrylakepublishing.com/activities.

CHAPTER THREE

Choosing Units

Ava will use equal amounts of each snack for her snack mix.

Ava is having friends over to play. She is making snacks to serve.

What food shall Ava give her friends? Ava wants to make a snack mix. She has peanuts, pretzels, raisins, and cereal squares.

Ava will make a quart of snack mix. A quart is a unit of measurement. One quart is two pints (0.9 L). Each pint is two cups (0.5 L).

That means one quart has four cups. Ava needs four cups of snack mix. There are four **ingredients**. She will use one cup (0.2 L) of each.

One cup (0.2 L) of each ingredient adds up to four cups total, or one quart (0.9 L).

Ava used cups to make the snack mix. Now she wants to add cinnamon. She needs a smaller unit of measurement.

Fluid ounces are small. There are eight fluid ounces in a cup (0.2 L). Tablespoons and teaspoons are even smaller. A tablespoon (15 mL) of butter melts in a frying pan. A teaspoon (5 mL) of vanilla goes in cookie batter.

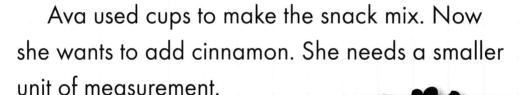

Ava measures cinnamon with a teaspoon.

1 Tbs

15ml

1 Tsp

5ml

Choose Your Units

Which units of volume could be used to measure these things? The first one is filled in for you.

Food for a kitten: _tablespoons_

Cough medicine in a bottle: _____

Paint for the walls: _____

Cinnamon in a recipe: _____

Shampoo in a bottle: _____

Water in a swimming pool: _____

Sand in a sandbox: _____

Juice for a snack: _____

To get a copy of this activity, visit www.cherrylakepublishing.com/activities.

STOP
Don't write in the book!

CHAPTER FOUR

Other Ways to Measure

Four quarts fit into one gallon.

Jack is thirsty! He has a gallon of milk. A gallon is a unit in the **U.S. customary system**. There are four quarts in a gallon (3.8 L).

Jack is making punch, too. The recipe uses quarts and liters. A liter is a bit bigger than a quart. You can buy two-liter bottles of soda at the store. The liter is a unit in the **metric system**. A shorter way to write liter is L. The metric system is another way to measure. It uses different units than the standard U.S. system. Milliliters are another unit in the metric system. There are 1,000 milliliters in a liter. A shorter way to write milliliter is mL.

Try measuring the ingredients for Jack's Purple Punch!

PURPLE PUNCH RECIPE
1 quart grape juice
2 liters ginger ale
Mix juice and ginger ale.
Add ice and stir.

Jack has two glasses. One glass is tall and narrow. One is short and wide. Can you guess which glass holds more punch?

Jack fills each glass with punch. He pours the punch from each glass into a measuring cup. Both glasses hold the same amount! Volume can be tricky. It is hard to guess how much liquid there is. That is why we measure instead of guessing.

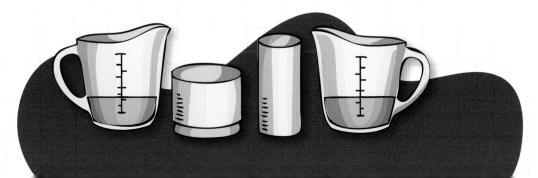

To get a copy of this activity, visit www.cherrylakepublishing.com/activities.

ACTIVITY

Fill a Jug

INSTRUCTIONS:

1. Gather three sizes of empty bottles: a gallon, a quart, and a liter.
2. First, place a funnel in the top of the gallon jug.
3. Then use the quart bottle to fill the gallon jug with water. How many quarts do you use to make a gallon?
4. Next, use the liter bottle to fill the gallon jug. Did the last liter fit? Which has more volume, a quart or a liter?

CHAPTER FIVE

Measuring Volume Is Fun!

Use cups to measure rice on a plate. Use quarts or liters to measure water in a goldfish bowl.

What is volume? It's how much space something takes up. How much water does a goldfish bowl hold? How much rice is on a plate? You can measure it to find out!

Here are more fun ways to measure volume:

- Scoop soil into a flowerpot with a measuring cup. How many cups does it take to fill the pot?

You can measure many types of food!

- Pour cereal into a glass measuring cup. What is the volume? Add milk and measure again.
- Pour one cup (0.2 L) of milk into a glass. Add a tablespoon (15 mL) of chocolate syrup. Stir it and take a sip. Is it chocolaty enough? If not, add more syrup, one teaspoon (5 mL) at a time. Yum!

Glossary

funnel (FUN-uhl) a hollow cone with a tube pointing down to direct flow into a small hole

ingredients (in-GREE-dee-ents) one of the parts of a mixture

metric system (MEH-trik SIS-tum) a way to measure things based on the number ten; the liter is used to measure volume

units (YOO-nits) standard amounts that are used to measure things

U.S. customary system (YOO-es KUS-tuh-mer-ee SIS-tum) units of measurement most often used in the United States such as cups, quarts, miles, feet, and inches

volume (VOHL-yume) the amount of space an object takes up

For More Information

BOOKS

Karapetkova, Holly. *Measuring: Pints, Gallons, and Quarts*. Rourke Publishing, 2011.

Karapetkova, Holly. *Measuring: Teaspoons, Tablespoons, and Cups*. Rourke Publishing, 2011.

Trumbauer, Lisa. *What is Volume?* New York: Children's Press, 2006.

Vogel, Julia. *Measuring Volume*. Mankato, MN: The Child's World, 2013.

WEB SITES

Math is Fun: Discover Capacity (Volumes)
http://www.mathsisfun.com/activity/discover-capacity.html
Find out how many ounces different kinds of cups and glasses around your house can hold. Then discover how many tablespoons each cup or glass holds.

PBS Kids: Can You Fill It?
http://pbskids.org/cyberchase/media/games/liquidvolume/
Choose from three pots to fill containers without spilling over. Fill each container in the fewest number of pours.

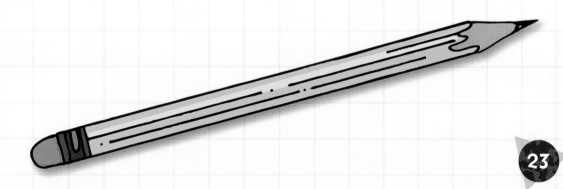

Index

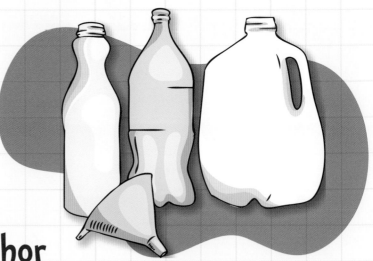

About the Author

Beth Bence Reinke has degrees in biology and nutrition. She is a registered dietitian, children's author, magazine writer, and a columnist for her favorite sport, NASCAR. When she's not writing, Beth enjoys measuring ingredients to bake muffins.